MAKING GODLY CHOICES
A DEVOTIONAL FOR TEENS

*A 7-Day Devotional to Help Teens Live
with Purpose and Faith*

RATONDREA O'NEAL
From Within Inspirations LLC

CONTENTS

ACKNOWLEDGMENTS

Thank you to my children, my family, and the many teens and leaders who inspired these pages. To every youth pastor, mentor, teacher, and parent who keeps showing up, your faithfulness matters. Thank you to the From Within Inspirations community for your encouragement and prayers.

A QUICK NOTE FOR TEENS

If you feel unsafe or pressured, talk to a trusted adult or leader right away. You are not alone.

Youth Leader Quick Start

Format:

Reading: 10 to 15 minutes

Discussion: 15 to 20 minutes

Prayer: 2 to 3 minutes

Facilitate: Ask open-ended questions. Let teens process. Do not rush silence.

Follow up: Send a midweek check-in and celebrate one small win.

ABOUT THE AUTHOR

Ratondrea O'Neal, founder of From Within Inspirations LLC, writes faith forward devotionals that help readers live Ephesians 6:11 and walk out their purpose. For teens, she breaks big choices into simple daily steps so you can put on God's armor, choose wisely, and stand strong at school, online, and with friends. Her Escape From Within series and 3AM Breakthroughs share hope, strength, and spiritual clarity drawn from her own journey with God.

Connect: Instagram @fromwithininspirations

Facebook: From Within Inspirations

Also, by From Within Inspirations:

Escape From Within (devotional)

Divine Detours (devotional series)

DEDICATION

For my son, Noah:

Your journey "from within" reminds me that God's foundation never fails. Even through struggle, His truth holds firm, His love leads steadily, and His purpose continues to shine through you.

> "Train up a child in the way he should go, and when he is old, he will not depart from it." Proverbs 22:6 (NIV)

I am proud of you, and I look forward to the man God is preparing you to be.

To every teen standing at the crossroads:

Remember: you are never too young to walk in wisdom, lead with faith, and shine for Christ.

INTRODUCTION

Do you ever notice how every day feels like a test?

People pull you one way, the world pulls another, and in the middle of it all, you are just trying to make the right move.

Making godly choices is not always easy. It means saying no when everyone else says yes. It means doing what is right, not just what is trending. And sometimes it means standing by yourself. But trust me, you are never really alone.

When you let God guide your choices, He keeps you from walking into things meant to break you. He helps you see past the moment into your purpose.

The Bible says, "In all your ways acknowledge Him, and He will make your paths straight" Proverbs 3:6 (NIV).

That means, before you act, before you post, before you speak, take a second to say, "God, what do You want me to do?"

WHY THIS BOOK

This devotional is a simple guide for real moments you face every day: peer pressure, relationships, social media, friendships, identity, your future, and forgiveness. In seven focused readings, you'll learn to pause, pray, and choose what honors God right where you are.

How to Use It

Start with prayer: Ask God to open your heart.

Read the Scripture slowly: Let it speak to your situation.

Sit with the message: Let the truth challenge and encourage you.

Be honest in reflection: There is no "perfect" answer, only your real one.

Pray: Pray the prayer or write your own.

Take the challenge: One faithful step at a time.

Use this on your own or with friends, family, or your youth group. Talk it out. Ask questions. Encourage each other. God meets us in the conversation.

Let's Pray

Lord, help me choose what honors You. Even when it is not cool, even when it is not easy, remind me that Your approval is the only one that really matters. In Jesus' name, Amen.

KEEP MAKING GODLY CHOICES, BECAUSE EVERY ONE OF THEM BUILDS THE LIFE HE HAS BEEN PLANNING JUST FOR YOU.

RATONDREA O'NEAL

Peer Pressure: When the Crowd Pulls Choosing Integrity Over Popularity

When friends want to do something, you know is not right (skipping class, vaping, gossiping, or disrespecting someone) the easy route is to go along.

Godly Choice: Stand firm in your values, even if it means standing alone.

DAY 1

WHEN THE CROWD PULLS

Choosing Integrity Over Popularity

Scripture Focus:

> "Do not conform to the pattern of this world, but be transformed by the renewing of your mind." Romans 12:2 (NIV)

Scenario:

Johnny's friends are skipping class to hang out behind the gym. They tell him, "Everyone does it, teachers don't even notice." Johnny hesitates. He doesn't want to look soft or "too good," but deep down, he knows it's wrong.

Devotional:

When everyone else is doing something, it's easy to go along just to fit in. But true strength is standing for what's right, even when you stand alone. Popularity fades, but character lasts. God calls you to be set apart, to make choices that reflect His light no matter who's watching.

Reflection:

When was the last time you felt pressured to go along with something you knew wasn't right? How did you respond?

_____

_____

_____

Prayer:

Lord, help me stand strong when it's hard to do the right thing. Give me courage to follow You, even when I feel alone. In Jesus' name, Amen.

Challenge:

This week, ask God for courage to say "no" when it's easier to say "yes."

Today's Truth: Standing alone with God is better than standing with a crowd without Him.

Ready to live it out? Today's Truth gives you a simple plan: grab the key truth, pick one real-life action, and walk one step with God today.

Scenario: Friends push Johnny to skip or vape.

Action Steps:

- **Right now:** Say a clear line: "Nah, I'm good," or "That's not me." Walk with one safe friend or text a parent or leader.

- **Next 24 hours:** Tell a trusted adult what happened, and plan a polite exit phrase for next time.

- **Ongoing habit:** Choose a "purpose buddy" who agrees to leave with you when things turn questionable.

- **If you slipped:** Own it before God (1 John 1:9), tell a mentor, and set a boundary for next time.

- **Resolution Line:** "My peace is worth more than your approval."

MY JOURNAL

_____
_____
_____
_____
_____
_____
_____
_____
_____
_____
_____
_____
_____
_____
_____
_____
_____
_____
_____
_____
_____
_____
_____
_____
_____
_____
_____
_____
_____
_____
_____
_____

RATONDREA O'NEAL

Group Discussion & Reflection

Use this space to talk through today's message whether you are in youth group, with friends, or with your family. Be open. Be honest. Be real. God works through conversation and connection.

Discussion Prompts

What part of today's devotional stood out most to you?

How can this Scripture help you make godly choices in your own life?

Was there a moment recently when you faced a similar situation? How did you handle it?

What's one thing you'll do differently after reading today's message?

How can this group pray for you this week?

Group Prayer (Optional):

Take a moment to pray together. Ask God to give everyone in your group wisdom and courage to live out today's lesson.

Relationships: When Feelings Get Deep Setting Boundaries in Dating

Teen years often bring first crushes and dating experiences. The challenge is balancing emotions with faith.

Godly Choice: Honor God in your relationships; seek purity, respect, and emotional wisdom.

DAY

2

WHEN FEELINGS GET DEEP

Setting Boundaries in Dating

Scripture Focus:

> "Above all else, guard your heart, for everything you do flows from it." Proverbs 4:23 (NIV)

Scenario:

Maya really likes her boyfriend. He's kind, funny, and tells her she's beautiful. But lately, he's been asking her to do things she's not comfortable with. She feels torn afraid to lose him, but afraid to lose herself too.

Devotional:

Dating can be exciting, but emotions can cloud judgment. God's plan for relationships is not to restrict you; it is to protect you. Healthy love starts with self-respect and clear boundaries rooted in faith. God wants you to protect your heart and your purpose. True love is built on respect and faith, not pressure or compromise.

Ask God to teach you how to honor Him in your relationships and to show you your worth through His eyes.

Reflection:

How can you honor God and yourself in the way you date or express interest in someone?

_____

_____

_____

Prayer:

God, thank You for loving me deeply. Help me see my value through You and build relationships that honor Your truth. Give me wisdom to know the difference between attraction and purpose. Amen.

Challenge:

Write three boundaries you can set to keep God at the center of your relationships.

_____

_____

_____

Today's Truth: Guarding your heart is not weakness; it is wisdom.

Ready to live it out? Today's Truth gives you a simple plan: grab the key truth, pick one real-life action, and walk one step with God today.

Scenario: Maya feels pressured by her boyfriend.

Action Steps:

Right now: Text or say, "I like you, but I'm not crossing this line." End the moment move to a public place, call a friend, or head home.

Next 24 hours: Write three boundaries (time, touch, talk). Share them with him. If they're not respected, step back.

Ongoing habit: Date in groups, during daylight, and in public places. Keep a curfew and stay connected with mentors.

If it's unhealthy: Break up kindly, clearly, and safely. Block if needed.

Resolution Line: "Respect me or release me."

MY JOURNAL

_____
_____
_____
_____
_____
_____
_____
_____
_____
_____
_____
_____
_____
_____
_____
_____
_____
_____
_____
_____
_____
_____
_____
_____
_____
_____
_____
_____
_____

RATONDREA O'NEAL

Group Discussion & Reflection

Use this space to talk through today's message whether you're in youth group, with friends, or with your family. Be open. Be honest. Be real. God works through conversation and connection.

Discussion Prompts

What part of today's devotional stood out most to you?

How can this Scripture help you make godly choices in your own life?

Was there a moment recently when you faced a similar situation? How did you handle it?

What's one thing you'll do differently after reading today's message?

How can this group pray for you this week?

Group Prayer (Optional):

Take a moment to pray together. Ask God to give everyone in your group wisdom and courage to live out today's lesson.

Social Media: When the Screen Speaks Reflecting Christ Online

Posting, commenting, or sharing online can either uplift or tear down.

Godly Choice: Think before you post. Represent Christ in how you communicate and respond.

DAY
3

WHEN THE SCREEN SPEAKS

Reflecting Christ Online

Scripture Focus:

"Let no corrupt talk come out of your mouths, but only what is helpful for building others up according to their needs." Ephesians 4:29 (NIV)

Scenario:

Jordan's group chat lights up after someone posts a meme mocking another student. Everyone reacts with laughing emojis. Jordan wants to fit in but can't shake the feeling that it's wrong to laugh at someone else's expense.

Devotional:

Your posts, comments, and shares tell a story about who you are. Before you post, pause and ask, "Does this represent Christ well?" Godly choices online can inspire, encourage, and remind others that kindness still matters. Social media can be a tool for connection or a trap for comparison. Use your voice to encourage, not tear down.

Reflection:

How can you use your online presence to spread kindness and faith?

_____

_____

_____

If someone only saw your social media, what would they learn about your faith?

_____

_____

_____

Prayer:

Jesus, help me to use my words and posts to honor You. Let everything, I share point people toward Your love. Amen.

Challenge:

Post or share one positive message, verse, or encouragement this week. Use your platform for purpose.

Today's Truth: What you post should point people closer to Christ, not further from Him.

Ready to live it out? Today's Truth gives you a simple plan: grab the key truth, pick one real-life action, and walk one step with God today.

Scenario: Group chat mocks a student.

Action Steps:

Right now: Don't react with emojis. DM the target a kind word. In the chat, set a boundary: "Hey, let's not do this."

Next 24 hours: Delete or unsend what you can. Apologize if you joined in. Mute or leave toxic threads.

Ongoing habit: Post using the Three-Question Filter. Set app limits and follow accounts that lift you up.

If targeted: Screenshot, report, and block. Tell a trusted adult.

Resolution Line: "If it doesn't build, I don't post."

MY JOURNAL

Group Discussion & Reflection

Use this space to talk through today's message whether you're in youth group, with friends, or as a family. Be open. Be honest. Be real. God works through conversation and connection.

Discussion Prompts:

What part of today's devotional stood out most to you?

How can this Scripture help you make better choices in your own life?

Was there a moment recently when you faced a similar situation? How did you handle it?

What's one thing you'll do differently after reading today's message?

How can this group pray for you this week?

Group Prayer (optional):

Take a moment to pray together. Ask God to give everyone in your group wisdom and courage to live out today's lesson.

Friendships: When Loyalty Costs You Choosing the Right Circle

Sometimes the people you call friends don't push you toward your purpose.

Godly Choice: Surround yourself with friends who encourage faith, not compromise.

WHEN LOYALTY COSTS YOU

Choosing the Right Friends

Scripture Focus:

> "**Do not be misled:** 'Bad company corrupts good character." 1 Corinthians 15:33 (NIV)

Scenario:

Brianna's been friends with the same crew since middle school. But lately, they've been gossiping, skipping youth group, and making fun of her for being "too churchy." She wonders if staying loyal to them is worth losing her peace.

Devotional:

Not everyone who calls you "friend" is meant to walk with you forever. Some relationships push you closer to God, while others pull you away. Godly choices mean choosing friends who strengthen your faith, not weaken it. Real friends lift you closer to God. Sometimes walking with Christ means walking away from people who pull you off track. Choosing the right friends is not about popularity, it's about peace and purpose. Pray for friends who challenge you to grow and love you as you are.

Reflection:

Who in your life helps you become more like Jesus?

_____

_____

_____

Do your closest friends encourage you to make better choices or compromise them?

_____

_____

_____

Prayer:

Lord, thank You for the gift of friendship. Help me build relationships that honor You, and give me wisdom to step away when needed. Amen.

Challenge:

Spend time with someone who inspires your faith this week. Pray for God to reveal which friendships need distance and which need deeper roots.

Today's Truth: Real friends help you grow closer to God, not away from Him.

Ready to live it out? Today's Truth gives you a simple plan: grab the key truth, pick one real-life action, and walk one step with God today.

Scenario: Brianna's crew mocks her faith.

Action Steps:

Right now: Name it calmly: "I'm not okay with being mocked." Change the subject or step away.

Next 24 hours: Spend time with one life-giving friend. Message a youth leader for guidance.

Ongoing habit: Map your circle: fuelers vs. drainers. Invest in fuelers. Limit time with drainers.

If they won't respect you: Create distance. You're not rude, you're healthy.

Resolution Line: "My friends should help me follow Jesus, not fight Him."

MY JOURNAL

Group Discussion & Reflection

Use this space to talk through today's message, whether you are in youth group, with friends, or as a family. Be open. Be honest. Be real. God works through conversation and connection.

Discussion Prompts:

What part of today's devotional stood out most to you?

How can this Scripture help you make better choices in your own life?

Was there a moment recently when you faced a similar situation? How did you handle it?

What's one thing you'll do differently after reading today's message?

How can this group pray for you this week?

Group Prayer (optional):

Take a moment to pray together. Ask God to give everyone in your group wisdom and courage to live out today's lesson.

Identity & Self-Worth: When You Forget Who You Are – Seeing Yourself Through God's Eyes

In a world that measures worth by likes, looks, and status, it's easy to forget who you are in Christ.

Godly Choice: Believe what God says about you, not what the world labels you.

DAY
5

WHEN YOU FORGET WHO YOU ARE

Seeing Yourself Through God's Eyes

Scripture Focus:

"I praise You because I am fearfully and wonderfully made; Your works are wonderful; I know that full well."
Psalm 139:14 (NIV)

Scenario:

Marcus scrolls through social media and feels smaller with every post. Everyone seems cooler, fitter, and more confident. He starts wishing he looked like them, forgetting who God created him to be.

Devotional:

The world will try to tell you who you should be, based on trends, looks, or likes. But your identity is not up for debate.

When you compare yourself to others, you lose sight of how God uniquely designed you. You are not an accident or a mistake you are His masterpiece. See yourself through His eyes: chosen, created with purpose, and loved without condition.

Reflection:

What's one thing you've believed about yourself that doesn't match what God says about you?

_____

_____

_____

Prayer:

Father, thank You for making me in Your image. Help me see my worth and walk confidently in Your purpose. Amen.

Challenge:

Write three truths from God's Word about who you are, and speak them daily.

_____

_____

_____

Today's Truth: You are more than enough because God made you on purpose and for a purpose.

Ready to live it out? Today's Truth gives you a simple plan: grab the key truth, pick one real-life action, and walk one step with God today.

Scenario: Marcus compares himself on social media.

Action Steps:

Right now: Close the app. Speak three truths: "I am chosen. I am called. I am enough in Christ."

Next 24 hours: Unfollow five comparison triggers. Write Psalm 139:14 where you'll see it.

Ongoing habit: Daily affirmations from Scripture; serve weekly and use your gifts (purpose > comparison).

If it returns: Repeat the truths out loud; text a friend to pray.

Resolution Line: "I do not chase likes; I live loved."

MY JOURNAL

RATONDREA O'NEAL

Group Discussion & Reflection

Use this space to talk through today's message, whether you are in youth group, with friends, or as a family. Be open. Be honest. Be real. God works through conversation and connection.

Discussion Prompts

What part of today's devotional stood out most to you?

How can this Scripture help you make better choices in your own life?

Was there a moment recently when you faced a similar situation? How did you handle it?

What's one thing you'll do differently after reading today's message?

How can this group pray for you this week?

Group Prayer (optional):

Take a moment to pray together. Ask God to give everyone in your group wisdom and courage to live out today's lesson.

Academic & Career Choices: When You Are Unsure What's Next Trusting God with the Future

Pressure to perform, pick a major, or meet expectations can create anxiety.

Godly Choice: Pray before you plan, trust God's timing and direction for your path.

DAY

6

WHEN YOU ARE UNSURE WHAT'S NEXT

Trusting God with Your Future

Scripture Focus:

> "In all your ways acknowledge Him, and He will make your paths straight." Proverbs 3:6 (NIV)

Scenario:

Tiana's friends already know what they want to be a doctor, an engineer, or an influencer but she has no clue. Her parents keep asking, "So what's next after graduation?" She prays but still feels uncertain about her path.

Devotional:

You do not have to have life all figured out. God's direction may not always be clear, but His timing is perfect. Trusting Him with your plans is the first step toward peace about your future.

It is normal to worry about what's next school, career, life after graduation but God already knows the path ahead. When you trust Him, He directs your steps. You do not need to see the whole map, just follow His voice one step at a time.

Reflection:

What's one area of your life where you need to trust God's plan more than your own?

_____

_____

_____

Prayer:

God, I give You my dreams and fears about the future. Guide me toward Your purpose and help me rest in Your timing. Amen.

Challenge:

Pray before you plan. Take one goal you are worried about and pray over it each day this week. Each morning, ask, "God, what do You want me to do today?"

Today's Truth: You do not have to know the plan when you know the Planner.

Ready to live it out? Today's Truth gives you a simple plan: grab the key truth, pick one real-life action, and walk one step with God today.

Scenario: Tiana feels behind.

Action Steps

Right now: Pray Proverbs 3:6 "God, lead my next step." Choose one small action (email a counselor, research one field).

Next 24 hours: Make a 30-day "Next Step Plan" (pray + explore + talk to two mentors + try one shadow/volunteer opportunity).

Ongoing habit: Weekly check-in with a mentor; journal open/closed doors; celebrate tiny progress.

If anxious: Breathe and shorten the horizon: "What faithful step can I take today?"

Resolution Line: "I do not need the whole map when I know the Guide."

MY JOURNAL

Group Discussion & Reflection

Use this space to talk through today's message whether you are in youth group, with friends, or as a family. Be open. Be honest. Be real. God works through conversation and connection.

Discussion Prompts

What part of today's devotional stood out most to you?

How can this Scripture help you make better choices in your own life?

Was there a moment recently when you faced a similar situation? How did you handle it?

What's one thing you'll do differently after reading today's message?

How can this group pray for you this week?

Group Prayer (optional):

Take a moment to pray together. Ask God to give everyone in your group wisdom and courage to live out today's lesson.

Forgiveness & Conflict: When You've Been Hurt Responding with Grace

Teens experience drama, misunderstandings, betrayal, bullying, and hurt.

Godly Choice: Choose forgiveness over revenge, even when it is hard.

WHEN YOU'VE BEEN HURT

Choosing Forgiveness Over Revenge

Scripture Focus:

> "Be kind and compassionate to one another, forgiving each other, just as in Christ God forgave you." Ephesians 4:32 (NIV)

Scenario:

Andre thought his best friend had his back. Then he found out that same friend was spreading rumors about him. The betrayal stings, and Andre's first thought is payback, but another voice reminds him there's a better way.

Devotional:

Being hurt by someone you trusted is painful. Holding on to pain keeps you stuck, but letting go invites healing.

Forgiveness does not mean forgetting, it means freeing yourself. It does not excuse what happened, but it releases you from the weight of anger. Godly choices turn pain into purpose when you choose forgiveness over bitterness.

Reflection:

Is there someone you need to forgive, or something you need to release, to move forward? How could you begin that process with God's help?

_____

_____

_____

Prayer:

Jesus, thank You for showing me what forgiveness looks like. Heal my heart and help me forgive like You. Amen.

Challenge:

Write a short prayer asking God to help you let go of anger and walk in peace. Write a short prayer for the person you are choosing to forgive.

_____

_____

_____

_____

_____

Today's Truth: Forgiveness frees your heart to heal and your life to move forward.

Ready to live it out? Today's Truth gives you a simple plan: grab the key truth, pick one real-life action, and walk one step with God today.

Scenario: Andre was betrayed.

Action Steps

Right now: Do not clap back. Step away and pray: "Jesus, guard my mouth and heal my heart."

Next 24 hours: Write a private forgiveness prayer. If it's wise and safe, set a boundary conversation: "That hurt. Here's my boundary."

Ongoing habit: Release daily in prayer, and replace bitter thoughts with blessings (Romans 12:21).

If they persist: Protect yourself set new boundaries, find a new circle, and involve adults if needed.

Resolution Line: "Forgiveness frees me; boundaries protect me."

MY JOURNAL

Group Discussion & Reflection

Use this space to talk through today's message, whether you are in youth group, with friends, or as a family. Be open. Be honest. Be real. God works through conversation and connection.

Discussion Prompts

What part of today's devotional stood out most to you?

How can this Scripture help you make better choices in your own life?

Was there a moment recently when you faced a similar situation? How did you handle it?

What's one thing you'll do differently after reading today's message?

How can this group pray for you this week?

Group Prayer (optional):

Take a moment to pray together. Ask God to give everyone in your group wisdom and courage to live out today's lesson.

MESSAGE FROM THE AUTHOR

KEEP CHOOSING GOD

Every day is filled with choices, some small, some big, all shaping who you are becoming.

When you choose what honors God, you invite His presence into your daily life.

You will not always get it right, but grace gives you a fresh start each time.

Keep praying. Keep listening. Keep growing.

And remember, godly choices do not just change your direction, they shape your destiny.

Keep walking in faith. Keep choosing God.

He's proud of the steps you are taking.

With love and purpose,

Ratondrea O'Neal, From Within Inspirations LLC

FROM WITHIN INSPIRATIONS TEEN

Make Godly Choices is part of the From Within Inspirations LLC collection, a series created to help teens grow in faith, strength, and purpose.

Follow @fromwithininspirations on Instagram for more messages of hope, strength, and spiritual breakthrough.

NOTES

"Your choices today build your tomorrow; choose God."

_____
_____
_____
_____
_____
_____
_____
_____
_____
_____
_____
_____
_____
_____
_____
_____
_____
_____
_____
_____
_____
_____
_____
_____